THE SPANISH
ARMADA

David Anderson

Hampstead Press New York 1988

Library of Congress Cataloging-in-Publication Data
Anderson, David, 1952 Aug. 22–
    The Spanish Armada / David Anderson.
        p.   cm. – (Armada)
    Includes Index.
    Summary: Describes the religious and territorial conflict between
England and Spain and discusses the events of 1588 when the Spanish
Armada met the English navy in the English Channel.
    ISBN 0-531-19505-8
    1. Armada. 1588–Juvenile literature. 2. Great Britain–History,
Naval–Tudors. 1485–1603–Juvenile literature. 3. Spain–History–
Philip II. 1556–1598–Juvenile literature. [1. Armada, 1588.
2. Great Britain–History, Naval–Tudors, 1485–1603. 3. Spain–
History–Philip II, 1556–1598.] I. Title. II. Series: Armada
(NewYork, N.Y.)
DA360.A57 1988
942.05′5–dc19

Title page: The Spanish Armada is presented as a dragon in this picture, which hangs in an English parish church. It was painted in about 1610, probably by one of the parishioners.

Contents page: An English shipwright works on ship plans at the time of the Armada. This picture was probably drawn by Matthew Baker, master shipwright at the Royal dockyard, in 1586.

Editor: Claire Llewellyn
Designer: James Marks
Picture research: Diana Morris
Production: Rosemary Bishop

Illustrators:
Paul Cooper: 4, 9, 10, 22–3t, 26t, 32,
    33l, 36l
Peter Dennis: 12–13
Graham Humphreys: 11, 14–15,
    16–17, 18–19, 20–21, 22–3b, 25,
    28–9, 34–5, 36–7

Photographs:
BPCC: 8b, 27b (Gemeentebibliotheek),
    43l, 45b
Bridgeman Art Library: 44t private
    collection
British Library: 18t
British Museum: 43r
R. M. Goodchild, courtesy of St Faith's
    Church, Gaywood: 30b (detail)
Courtesy of the Hispanic Society, New
    York: 6t
Lausanne Museum: 9t (detail)

By permission of the Master and
    Fellows, Magdalene College,
    Cambridge: Contents page
MAS, by courtesy of Excma Sra
    Duquesa de Medina Sidonia: 12
Municipal Museum "de Lakenhal,"
    Leiden: 28b
Musées Royaux des Beaux-Arts de
    Belgique: 13
Museo Naval, Madrid: 16
National Maritime Museum: endpapers,
    5b, 7t, 10t, 11b, 19, 22, 26–7, 27t
    (detail), 28t, 30t, 33t, 42, 44b
Collection Art Gallery of New South
    Wales: 45t ("The Armada in Sight,"
    John Seymour Lucas 1880)
Rijksmuseum, Amsterdam: 31
Courtesy of the Marquess of Salisbury:
    7b
Scottish National Portrait Gallery: 8t
Staatliche Kunstammlungen, Kassel: 5t
The Ulster Museum, Belfast: 38–9,
    40–41

The author and publishers would like to
thank Colin Martin for generously
giving them access to his research, and
for his invaluable comments on Armada
wrecks. They are also grateful to Dr Mia
Rodriguez-Salgado for her advice
throughout the project; and to Lawrence
Flanagan for supplying information
about the Armada in Ireland.

    Particular thanks are also due to the
following members of staff at the
National Maritime Museum for their
help and encouragement: Dr Stephen
Deuchar, Ian Friel, Dr Roger Knight
and John Palmer. For their assistance,
thanks are also due to David Lyon, Dr
Alan McGowan and David White; also
to Margaret Hudson and Jane Wright
for typing the text, and to all the other
Museum staff who valuably contributed
their help.

    Finally, the author also wishes to thank
his wife, Josphine Anderson, for her
advice and support.

CONTENTS

ELIZABETH I AND ENGLAND

△ The coat-of-arms of Mary I of England and Philip II of Spain. Mary was a Catholic. She married Philip in 1554 to form an alliance between England and Catholic Spain.

▽ The family tree of the royal families of England, Scotland and Spain. Until the 1560s, England and Spain were often on friendly terms.

Elizabeth I became Queen of England in 1558. At that time England was a poor and backward country. It had a small population with probably no more than three or four million people. There were no large cities apart from London. Most of the people lived and worked on the land. They looked after herds of cattle and sheep or grew crops. When the harvest failed many of the poorest people died from starvation and disease.

In the sixteenth century (1500–1599), most people in Europe were Christians. By the 1580s they were divided into two opposing groups, Catholics and Protestants. Catholics believed that the Catholic church, with the Pope in Rome as its leader, was the only true Church. But Protestants refused to accept the Pope's leadership and set up their own independent churches. Elizabeth was a devout Protestant and she knew that most of her people favored the Protestant religion. So when she became Queen, she decided to make England a Protestant country. Within 30 years, the most important people in Elizabeth's court were fiercely Protestant, and England was the leading Protestant country in Europe.

People respected the Queen both at home and abroad. She was a cautious and capable ruler, who disliked risky policies and who disliked spending money even more! She listened to the advice of her ministers, but she made every important decision herself. Even the Catholic Pope, Sixtus V, admired her. "Just look how well she governs!" he said. "She is only a woman, only mistress of half an island, yet she makes herself feared by Spain, by France, by Empire, by all."

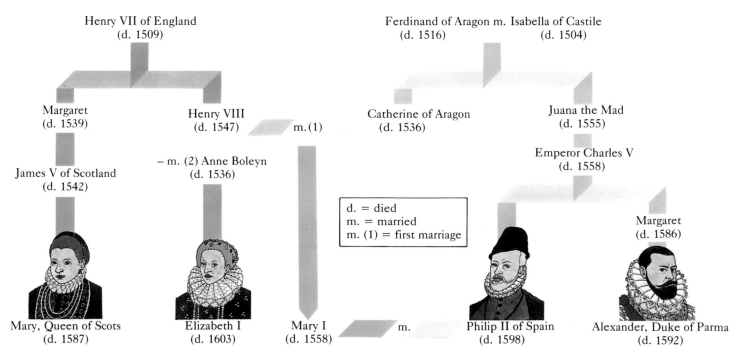

Henry VII of England
(d. 1509)

Ferdinand of Aragon m. Isabella of Castile
(d. 1516)   (d. 1504)

Margaret
(d. 1539)

Henry VIII
(d. 1547)   m.(1)

Catherine of Aragon
(d. 1536)

Juana the Mad
(d. 1555)

James V of Scotland
(d. 1542)

– m. (2) Anne Boleyn
(d. 1536)

Emperor Charles V
(d. 1558)

d. = died
m. = married
m. (1) = first marriage

Margaret
(d. 1586)

Mary, Queen of Scots
(d. 1587)

Elizabeth I
(d. 1603)

Mary I
(d. 1558)   m.

Philip II of Spain
(d. 1598)

Alexander, Duke of Parma
(d. 1592)

4

◁ Elizabeth took a close interest in England's relations with other countries. In this painting, she is meeting Dutch envoys from the Protestant part of the Netherlands. The Dutch often sent envoys to ask Elizabeth to give them money for their fight against Catholic Spain.

Elizabeth was careful to create an image of wealth and power to impress her own citizens as well as foreigners. She knew that she depended on the loyalty of ordinary people and she was always at her best when she appeared in public. In her speeches she proclaimed her Englishness and her love for the crowds who lined the streets. Of course, only a few English men or women ever met the Queen in person, or heard her speak. But many more people heard flattering descriptions of her which were read from pamphlets that were sold all over the country.

▽ Greenwich Palace was Queen Elizabeth's favorite palace outside London. She was born here and loved to sit in the orchards and gardens. She also liked to hunt in the park nearby. Elizabeth enjoyed all the entertainments of court life: music, dancing, games of chess and cards and, of course, good company.

PHILIP II AND SPAIN

△ Philip was devoted to his children. His daughter Isabella (*left*) often sat beside him in his study as he worked. She dried the ink on his papers and passed him new documents to read.

Philip of Spain was the most powerful ruler in the world. As well as being King of Spain, he owned large areas of Europe and most of Central and South America. He had inherited this vast empire from his parents. In Spain alone Philip ruled over eight million people. The wealth of the Spanish empire was enormous. America provided Philip with huge amounts of gold and silver. In Europe, the richest country in the empire was the Netherlands, which was famous for its merchants and its trade.

Spain should have been a very wealthy country. It was not. Some of the people in the Protestant part of the Netherlands were rebelling against Spanish rule. The Spanish army was fighting the rebels, and Philip was using most of his gold and silver from America to pay for the war. As time went on, the Spanish government needed more and more money. It began to borrow huge sums of money from foreign banks and from its own people at high rates of interest. Spanish citizens preferred to make money in this way rather than invest it in Spain's trade and industries. As a result, trade in Spain suffered.

Almost every day, Philip sat at a desk in one of his palaces, and worked his way through a mountain of papers from all over his empire. Unlike Elizabeth, he disliked company. He found it difficult to trust his ministers and was very careful not to show his feelings in public. His greatest pleasure was to be alone. The king loved gardening. He spent much of his spare time in his gardens and he loved to supervise the planting of trees and flowers. At each of his palaces, Philip made sure that his desk looked out on to the gardens. He also loved books, music and paintings.

Philip was a Catholic and a deeply religious man. He spent long hours in prayer. When he built a new palace, the Escorial, he made sure that it had a monastery as well. His bedroom was next to the chapel, so that he could hear the services when he was lying in bed. Philip was devoted to the Catholic faith and he firmly believed that God was on his side in any war against Protestants.

△ In 1571 the Spanish led a fleet of ships from Catholic countries which defeated a powerful Turkish fleet at the Battle of Lepanto. After Lepanto, Philip had more time to plan his war in the Netherlands.

△ Philip's favorite palace was the Escorial, in the mountains near Madrid. It was quiet and remote. Philip supervised much of the building work himself, and when it was finished he said it was "the lady of his heart." He loved the palace so much that, during his last illness in 1598, he came to the Escorial to die.

The drawing (*above*) shows the palace at the time it was being built.

WAR IN EUROPE

△ On Elizabeth's orders, Mary, Queen of Scots was eventually executed in February 1587. Mary passed to Philip her claim to the English throne.

▽ By 1588 Philip had a huge army of 63,000 men in the Netherlands who were fighting against the Dutch rebels. Elizabeth was afraid that the army could easily cross the Channel and attack England.

In Europe, in the 1580s, the differences between the two religious groups, Catholics and Protestants, caused great bitterness. Spain was the strongest Catholic country, and England was the leading Protestant country.

In England, the Catholics were in a very difficult position. In 1570 the Pope ordered all English Catholics to disobey Queen Elizabeth and to help ovethrow her. Most Catholics were loyal to the Queen but they still wanted to follow their religion. Now they had to make a choice between the two. Many of them were imprisoned. During the next 30 years, the English government tortured and executed more than 200 Catholics.

Protestants in Spain were also persecuted. They were usually handed over to the Spanish Inquisition. This was a religious court which found and punished people who were not Catholic. Like the English government, the Inquisition sometimes used torture. In serious cases, the punishment was death by burning.

In France, religious differences led to civil war between the Catholics and Protestants in the 1560s. France had once been the most powerful country in Europe; so powerful, that England and Spain had made an alliance to protect themselves. Now that France

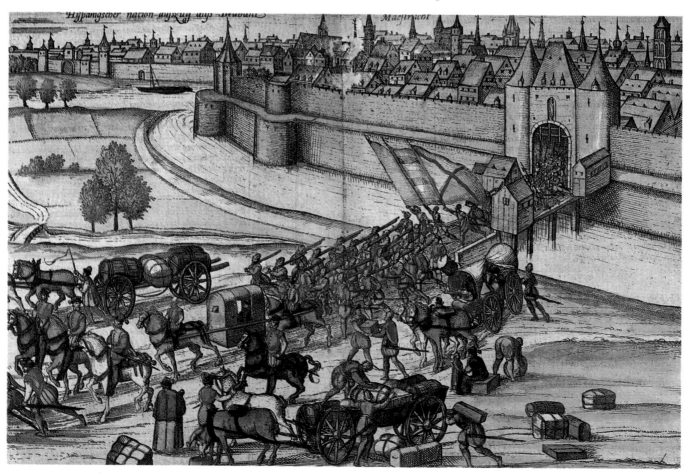

was less of a danger, England and Spain no longer needed their alliance. The two countries gradually became enemies.

Philip II was looking for ways of weakening Elizabeth's power. He knew that she faced dangers from both Ireland and Scotland. Ireland was an English colony but most of the people there were Catholic. Some of the Irish lords asked Philip to overthrow the English. Scotland was a different problem. Scotland's former queen, Mary, was Elizabeth's prisoner. Mary was a Catholic and she was Elizabeth's closest relative. Some English Catholics wanted to kill Elizabeth and make Mary Queen of England. But if Elizabeth executed Mary for treason, she then risked a Scottish invasion.

Philip had troubles of his own in the Netherlands, where Dutch Protestants were rebelling against Spanish rule. The Netherlands coast is less than 100 miles from England. Elizabeth was afraid that if Philip defeated the Dutch rebels, he would use his army to attack England. In 1585 she decided to send an army of 7000 English soldiers to fight against the Spanish army in the Netherlands. This action angered Philip. For the first time England and Spain were openly at war.

△ Protestants and Catholics in France were bitter enemies. On August 24, 1584, Catholics in Paris murdered 3,000 Protestants in what became known as the "St. Bartholomew's Day Massacre."

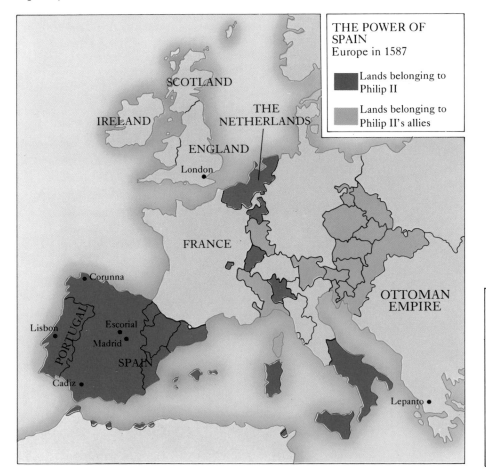

THE POWER OF SPAIN
Europe in 1587

■ Lands belonging to Philip II

□ Lands belonging to Philip II's allies

SCOTLAND
IRELAND
THE NETHERLANDS
ENGLAND
London
FRANCE
Corunna
Lisbon
Escorial
Madrid
PORTUGAL
Cadiz
SPAIN
OTTOMAN EMPIRE
Lepanto

◁ This map shows the strength of Spain. In 1587 the lands that belonged to Philip II and his allies covered half of Europe. England's only allies were the Dutch rebels.

IMPORTANT EVENTS IN EUROPE

1562 Civil war begins in France.
1566 Dutch Protestants rebel against Spanish rule.
1570 The Pope orders English Catholics to disobey Elizabeth.
1572 St Bartholomew's Day Massacre.
1585 Elizabeth sends an English army to the Netherlands.
1587 Mary, Queen of Scots is executed.

PRIVATEERS

△ The silver mines at Potosi. The Spanish settlers forced the native Indians to work in the silver mines in America. Large numbers of them died from ill treatment and disease.

▽ The Spanish conquered Central and South America in order to plunder its treasure. By 1588, Spanish ships were bringing back two million ducats-worth of silver each year.

Spain's empire in America was Philip's most valuable possession. Each summer, ships set out from Spain with their holds full of wine, oil, cloth and tools to sell to the Spanish settlers in Central and South America. The following autumn, the same ships came back full of treasures from the silver mines. Philip used most of this money to pay for his army in the Netherlands. Without it, Spain would be bankrupt.

Philip claimed that all America belonged to Spain. He tried to stop ships of any other country from trading with his American colonies or landing people to settle there. But many European countries, including England, did not accept these claims. They wanted to trade with the Spanish settlers and have a share of the American treasure.

Before long, privateers began to sail the seas between America and Spain. The privateers were English, French or Dutch seamen with fast, well-armed ships. They carried documents from their governments which allowed them to attack and capture the Spanish treasure ships and take them back to their home ports. The privateers made large profits for themselves, and anyone else who helped pay for the venture. The Spanish government took no notice of the documents that the privateers carried and regarded them as no better than pirates. It was forced to group its ships into convoys, and protect them with a special fleet of fighting ships.

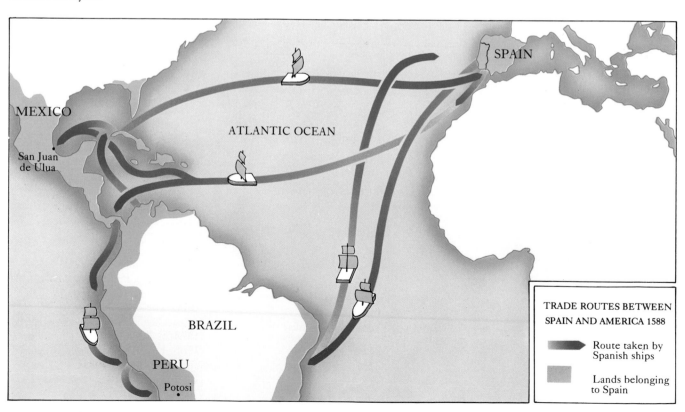

MEXICO

San Juan de Ulua

ATLANTIC OCEAN

SPAIN

BRAZIL

PERU

Potosi

TRADE ROUTES BETWEEN SPAIN AND AMERICA 1588

Route taken by Spanish ships

Lands belonging to Spain

◁ Drake raided Cadiz in April 1587. The townspeople watched in fury as he destroyed 24 Spanish ships in the harbor. The ships were all loaded with supplies for the Spanish fleet. The raid stopped Philip from attacking England that year.

The privateer the Spanish feared most was an Englishman, Francis Drake. In 1568 Drake and his cousin, John Hawkins, sailed to America to sell slaves to the Spanish settlers. Philip had forbidden all foreigners to trade in America, and Spanish naval patrols guarded the ports. At the port of San Juan de Ulua a Spanish patrol saw the English ships. At first the patrol agreed to let Drake and Hawkins go free, but then it started to fire on them without warning. The Englishmen only just managed to escape. After that, Drake took every opportunity to attack the Spanish. He seemed to find Spanish ships by instinct. The Spanish said he had a magic mirror and could see all the oceans of the world and all the ships that sailed on them.

Drake's personal war against Spain continued into the 1580s. By 1587 the English believed that Philip was preparing a fleet to invade England. Elizabeth ordered Drake to spoil Philip's plans, and he led an outrageous but successful attack on the port of Cadiz. Back home, Drake boasted that he had "singed the King of Spain's beard." Even Philip had to admit that the raid was very daring. But he was determined to end these English attacks.

△ Francis Drake became very famous in Europe. In 1588 crowds flocked to see his portrait when it was put on display in Italy.

PHILIP'S INVASION PLAN

By January 1586 Philip had made the decision to invade England. This was his plan. The Spanish army in the Netherlands was led by the Duke of Parma, the most able general in Europe. Philip could use this army to attack England. The army would need protection as it sailed across the English Channel. Philip would send a fleet from Spain to provide this protection – an Armada, commanded by the brilliant admiral, the Marquis of Santa Cruz. The Armada would carry all the equipment needed for a land war: massive siege guns to smash the walls of towns and castles; horses and mules to pull carriages; tents for the officers; knapsacks for the men, and so on. The fleet would also carry an extra 20,000 soldiers to join Parma's army.

Philip did not really expect his invasion force to conquer England. But he hoped to force Elizabeth to agree to three demands. Most important, Elizabeth must end the persecution of English Catholics. Next, she must stop helping the Dutch rebels. Lastly, she must pay Philip the full cost of the invasion.

1 The Armada would sail from Spain, up the English Channel, to the Netherlands. It had orders to fight the English fleet only if it was attacked.

△ This portrait of the Duke of Medina Sidonia was painted in his old age. He was only 38 when the Armada sailed.

3 The Spanish army would cross the Channel to England. The Armada would protect it from attacks by the English fleet. Philip wanted Parma to land his men on the north coast of Kent. They would unload all their equipment from the ships. Next they would march to London and try to capture the city.

△ The Duke of Parma was Philip's nephew and the greatest general of the age. The invasion of England could not succeed without his army.

2 When the Armada reached the Netherlands it would anchor in deep water a few miles from the coast. Parma's army would then cross the shallow water near the coast in barges and join the Armada out at sea.

In 1586 and throughout the spring of 1587, Admiral Santa Cruz prepared the Spanish fleet to sail that summer. Guns were made, men were recruited and ships were quickly gathered together from all around Spain and from Spain's allies in Europe. But in April 1587 Drake raided Cadiz. The attack destroyed large quantities of food and weapons. Philip had to delay the invasion until the next year.

In February 1588 Philip's plans received another blow: Santa Cruz died. Philip chose the Duke of Medina Sidonia to be the fleet's new commander. He was a good choice. He was an excellent organizer, and during the campaign he showed great courage and leadership.

AN ARMADA SUPPLY SHIP

The Armada had two important purposes: it had to carry the Spanish army and it was a battle fleet. It needed huge amounts of food and equipment, because the campaign would last for many months. This was a problem for the Armada's commanders. There was simply not enough room in the holds of the fighting ships to carry all these supplies. So they gathered together a squadron of 23 ships to carry the supplies. Some of these cargo ships, called hulks, had special uses: two were outfitted as hospital ships and others carried horses and mules.

Most of the hulks for the Armada came from ports on the Baltic coast of Germany. In peacetime they carried timber, tar, grain, metal and canvas from Eastern Europe to Spain. Now they would carry supplies for the Armada. The hulks were barrel-like ships, which were slow and clumsy to sail. They had few guns and could not defend themselves against an enemy in a sea battle. They had to rely on the Armada's fighting ships to protect them.

▷ The *Gran Grifon* from Rostock in Germany was the flagship of the hulks. In March 1587 it carried a cargo of timber to Spain and then joined the Armada. During the next year, until the Armada sailed, Spanish clerks kept careful records of every item on board, for example (*see right*):

   1 Meat (mainly bacon)
   2 Leather shoes in baskets
   3 Knapsacks (for use on land)
   4 Hand lanterns
   5 Jars (for wine or olive oil)
   6 Barrels containing drinking water
There were also 43 sailors and 243 soldiers on board.

This drawing of the *Gran Grifon's* cargo is based on these records. The *Gran Grifon* never returned from the Armada campaign. It was very badly damaged during the battles with the English fleet, and it eventually sank off Fair Isle in September 1588.

6

15

THE ARMADA SAILS

Philip believed that Spain was fighting a holy war for the Catholic faith. It would succeed with God's help. On April 25, 1588, the Duke of Medina Sidonia took the fleet's banner to be blessed in Lisbon Cathedral. The Duke also ordered every soldier, sailor, officer and slave to confess his sins to a priest before sailing. No one was to swear or gamble. The crew of each ship had to say prayers before the mainmast each morning and evening during the campaign.

A few weeks before the Armada left Lisbon the Spanish government did something extraordinary. It published a detailed description of the fleet and distributed it throughout Europe. English spies had been trying to gather this information for months! Now Elizabeth's ministers knew that there were 130 ships in the Spanish fleet, with 18,937 soldiers, 8,050 sailors and 2,088 slaves. The report even described how many guns there were on each ship, and how much powder and shot. The Spanish must have believed that this description of their great fleet would frighten the English.

On May 30 "La Felicissima Armada," the "Most Fortunate Fleet," sailed from Lisbon. Storms forced it into the northern Spanish port of Corunna for repairs and fresh food. It was not until July 22 that it finally left for England.

△ A sixteenth-century model of a galleon from a church in Spain. The relatives and friends of Spanish sailors prayed in front of models like this one for the safety of the men while they were at sea.

▷ Three different kinds of ships in the Armada. The **galleons** (*center*) were the front-line fighting ships of Philip's navy. They carried the best and heaviest guns. The **merchant ships** (*rear left*) were from all over Europe, not just Spain. Some were forced to join the Armada when they docked at a Spanish port. The **galleasses** (*right*) used both oars and sails to drive them through the water.

PREPARATIONS FOR THE ARMADA

January 1586 Philip decides to invade England.

April 1587 Drake's raid on Cadiz.

February 1588 Santa Cruz dies. Medina Sidonia is appointed commander.

May 1588 The Armada leaves Lisbon.

July 1588 The Armada leaves Corunna.

ENGLISH PREPARATIONS

△ This painting shows fire beacons on the Dorset coast. All over England, villages near the beacons took turns sending men to keep watch.

In 1586 Elizabeth's ministers heard rumors that Philip intended to invade England. At once they started to prepare the country's defenses.

Government officials were highly suspicious of the English Catholics. They were afraid that some Catholics secretly supported the Spanish and would help the invasion. No Catholics were allowed to help with the defense of the country, and in 1588 many priests and other Catholics were put into prison or kept under house arrest.

Ordinary people had an important part to play in the war if the Spanish army landed. England had a network of fire beacons all over the country. Day and night, villagers stood ready to light their beacons as soon as the Armada reached England. This was the signal for church bells to ring out, and for local militias to get their guns and pikes. In London young boys formed their own cadet force. They chose officers, marched with drums and even practiced with half-sized weapons.

Of course, the local militias alone could not defeat the powerful Spanish army. The government also had three large armies: one in the North to stop an invasion by the Scots; another in London to protect Elizabeth; and the largest at Tilbury, in Essex, to guard the mouth of the Thames.

England's main defense was its fleet. Some of the ships in the fleet belonged to the Queen, but most of them were English merchant ships, which were called up on the Queen's orders. Since 1578 John Hawkins had been responsible for the repair of the Queen's ships. He had done a good job. But the crews themselves were in poor shape. In the summer of 1588 sickness spread through the fleet. On one ship, the *Elizabeth Bonaventure,* 200 men died in just three weeks. Worse still, many of the healthy men wanted to desert. They hadn't been paid for months because the Queen was short of money. If the Armada was coming, Elizabeth's ministers hoped it would come soon.

△ John Hawkins was one of the most experienced of the English commanders.

◁ An Elizabethan ship under construction. Changes were made to the design of the Queen's ships in the 1580s. These made the ships faster and able to change direction more quickly than the Spanish ships.

△ Lord Howard of Effingham, the Lord Admiral of the English Fleet.

LIFE AT SEA

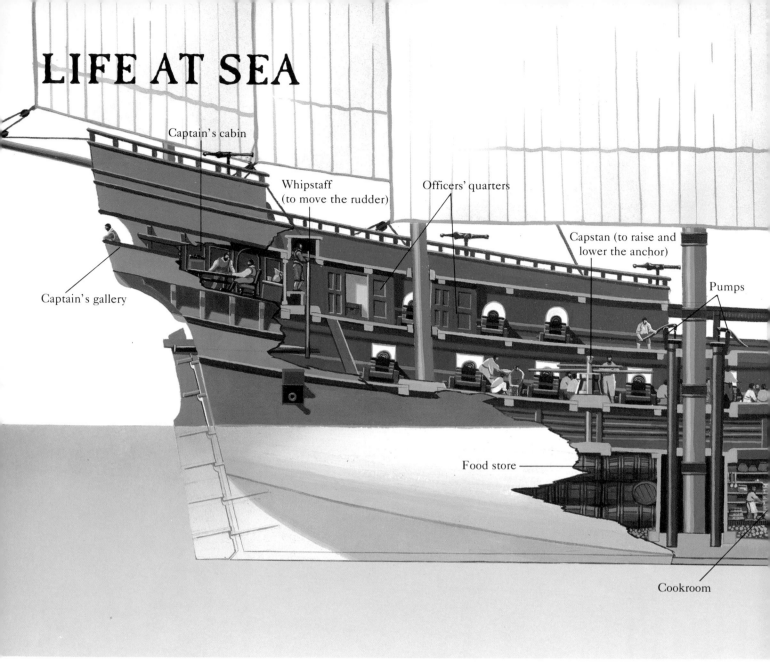

Captain's cabin

Whipstaff
(to move the rudder)

Officers' quarters

Capstan (to raise and
lower the anchor)

Pumps

Captain's gallery

Food store

Cookroom

△ Inside a fast-sailing English fighting ship, a "race-built galleon." The drawing shows how some parts of the ship were probably used. We cannot be certain because no English ship plans have survived. The hold was the dirtiest and smelliest part of the ship. It may be surprising to us today to learn that food was stored there. Also, during a battle, wounded men were brought there to leave the decks clear for the fighting. The captain's and officers' cabins were on the upper decks, where they enjoyed plenty of fresh air and light. The cabins had wood paneling to keep out the rats and mice.

Half the crew of a sixteenth-century ship often died by the end of any long voyage. But a sailor was more likely to die after eating his dinner than from gunshot wounds. Food poisoning, scurvy and diseases such as typhus and dysentery were the most common killers. In 1588 the Spanish fleet had two hospital ships and 93 doctors, surgeons and other medical staff. It was better prepared than the English fleet, which had no hospital ships and only a few surgeons. When men died, their bodies were thrown over the side of the ship.

Life on board ship for the ordinary sailor was hard. The men were usually cold and wet and had no fires to warm them. Their food was stored in the hold, and this was the filthiest part of the ship. Rats and mice scurried over the food, worms wriggled in the biscuits, and fleas and lice infested the sailors' clothes. Meat was often rotten and drinking water was green.

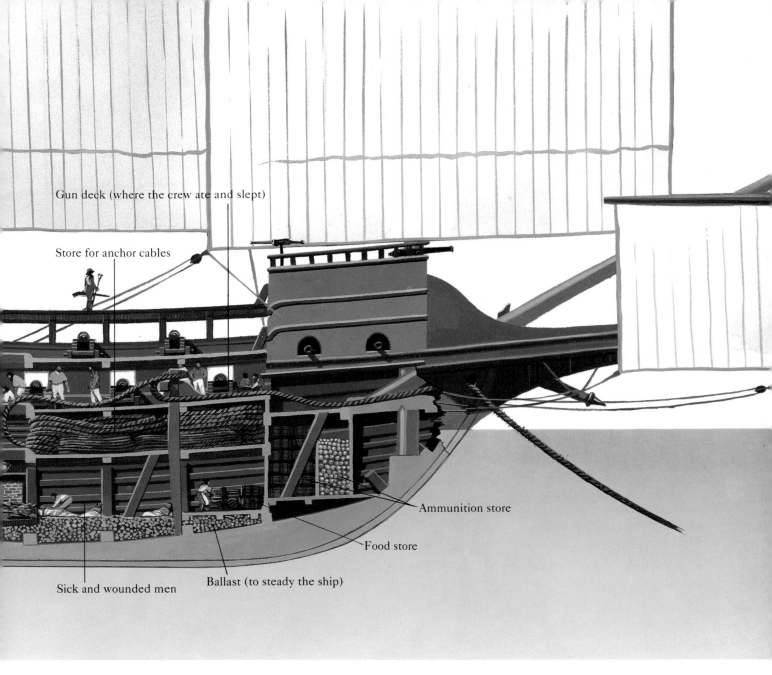

Gun deck (where the crew ate and slept)

Store for anchor cables

Ammunition store

Food store

Sick and wounded men

Ballast (to steady the ship)

It was no wonder that few sailors wanted to join the navy for a long voyage. To make up a full crew, men were pressed into the fleet by force, or by the threat of imprisonment. The officers complained that their men were the dregs of the earth: they swore, gambled and were highly superstitious.

The officers lived a little more comfortably than the men. On a large English ship the captain lived in a cabin with glass windows, damask curtains and wooden furniture. Other officers had their own cabins, but these only had room for a bed and a few personal possessions. Officers had to pay for any extra luxury with their own money. On some of the Armada ships, the grandest gentlemen wore perfumed clothes of embroidered satin and velvet, with gold and silver lace and gold buttons. They sat down to dinner at tables lit by candles in silver candlesticks, and ate and drank from plates and goblets of solid silver and gold.

"*It is a privilege of the galley that the meat that is normally eaten there should be dried goat meat, quarters of sheep, salt beef and rusty bacon. This must be parboiled and not boiled, lightly burnt and not roasted, in such a way that, set on the table, it is loathsome to look at, hard as the devil to gnaw at, salty as hell to eat, indigestible as stones, and harmful as rat poison if you eat your fill.*"

This is an extract from a humorous sixteenth-century book, *The Art of Sailing*, written by a Spanish bishop.

BATTLES IN THE CHANNEL

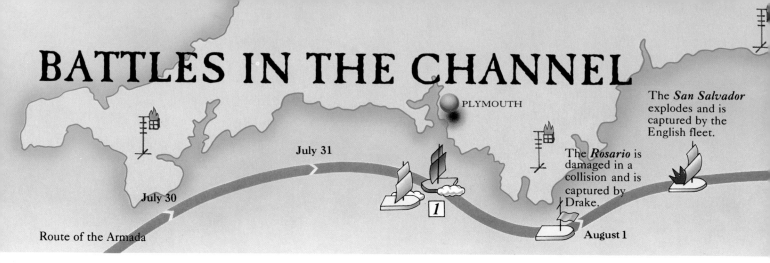

PLYMOUTH

July 31

July 30

Route of the Armada

The *San Salvador* explodes and is captured by the English fleet.

The *Rosario* is damaged in a collision and is captured by Drake.

August 1

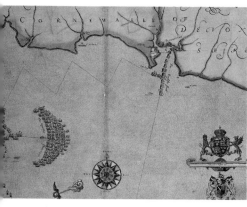

△ The Spanish battle formation was purely defensive. The strong fighting ships were put on the wings of the crescent. The weaker ships, such as the hulks, were in the middle.

On Friday July 29, an English patrol ship spotted the Armada about 100 miles from Plymouth. Within hours, row boats were towing the English fleet out of Plymouth harbor, and fire beacons were spreading the alarm to London and the north of England. On the following day the two fleets faced each other for the first time.

The Armada's commander, Medina Sidonia, fired a gun as a signal to his ships. The English sailors then watched in amazement as the Spanish fleet moved into its battle formation. The ships grouped together in the shape of a crescent that spread several miles from wing to wing. It must have been a terrifying sight. No fleet had ever used a formation like this before. But Lord Howard,

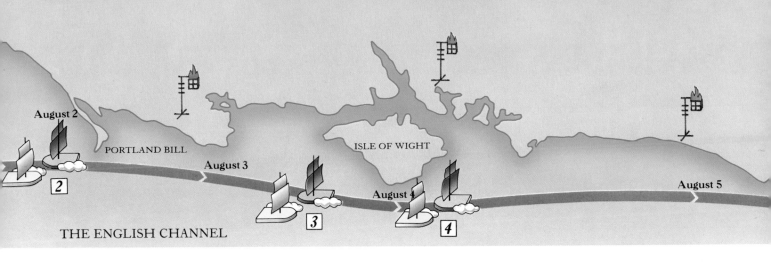

August 2

PORTLAND BILL

August 3

ISLE OF WIGHT

August 4

August 5

2

3

4

THE ENGLISH CHANNEL

△ A map of the south coast of England which shows the sites of the four battles in the Channel:
1 Plymouth – July 31
2 Portland Bill – August 2
3 Isle of Wight – August 3
4 Isle of Wight – August 4

the English commander, knew he had two advantages over the Spanish fleet: faster ships and a larger number of long-range guns. Howard decided not to attack the Armada yet, but to follow it from a safe distance.

During the next week, as the Armada sailed up the Channel, there were four sea battles between the two fleets. Yet by the time the Armada reached Calais, not a single English or Spanish ship had been sunk by enemy fire, and only a few hundred men were dead. Each battle had ended in stalemate.

◁ On July 30, the English sailors caught their first sight of the huge Spanish fleet as it sailed toward them in the late afternoon sun.

WAR AT SEA

△ Spanish sea guns had carriages with only two wheels. They were difficult to move and difficult to aim. The English guns were easier and quicker to load and fire because their carriages had four wheels.

During the sea battles between the English and Spanish fleets, the two sides fired at each other continuously but inflicted very little damage. They used up huge quantities of powder and shot.

The English gunners were able to fire their guns three times faster than the Spanish. There were several reasons for this. The English had the finest guns and the best-trained gunners in Europe. English ships also carried more guns than the Spanish ships, which had to use space to store food and equipment. Above all, the design of English gun carriages allowed the gunners to clean, reload and aim their guns very quickly.

The battle tactics of the two fleets were quite different. At first, the English commanders believed they could win the war with their long-range guns; they would sink the Spanish ships one by one from a safe distance. These tactics failed because sixteenth-century guns were difficult to aim and were too unreliable to do any real damage.

The Spanish commanders did not plan to win a battle with their guns alone. The Armada's strength was that it carried a large number of tough and well-trained soldiers, who were armed with muskets, arquebuses, pikes and swords. If an English ship got too close, the Spanish commanders intended to pull it alongside with grappling hooks and then send the soldiers on board to capture it. But the English ships were too nimble to be caught in this way, and the Spanish never got the chance to try out their tactics.

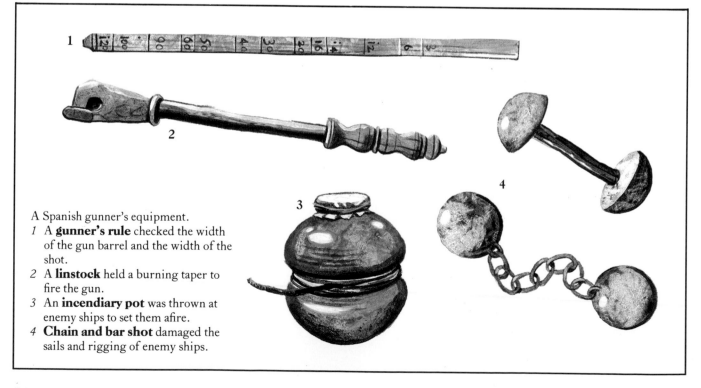

A Spanish gunner's equipment.
1 A **gunner's rule** checked the width of the gun barrel and the width of the shot.
2 A **linstock** held a burning taper to fire the gun.
3 An **incendiary pot** was thrown at enemy ships to set them afire.
4 **Chain and bar shot** damaged the sails and rigging of enemy ships.

▽ English guns in action. The gun
crew first cleaned out the barrel of the
gun. Then they ladled in the powder
and the shot. They packed the barrel
with wadding to keep everything in
place. When the master gunner aimed
the gun, one of the crew fired. He held
a burning taper next to the touch hole.
This lit the powder and the gun fired.

25

FIRESHIPS AT CALAIS

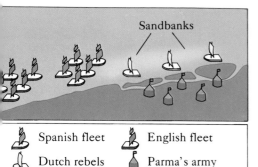

Sandbanks

Spanish fleet · English fleet · Dutch rebels · Parma's army

△ On August 6 the Armada anchored close to Calais. The English fleet watched and waited. Rebel Dutch ships were ready to attack Parma's army if he tried to sail out to join the Armada.

▷ The fireships at Calais. The English were lucky that the wind and tide were both in the right direction to send the fireships toward the Spanish fleet. Wooden ships carried little defense against fire. The Armada ships had piles of old sails and clothes. Their crews were ready to soak these and throw them over small fires. But this was no protection from the fireships, so the Spanish fled.

As the Armada completed its journey up the English Channel, the commanders of both fleets were anxious and uncertain about what would happen next.

The English commander, Lord Howard, knew that his fleet had failed to break the Armada's strong crescent formation. His ships were now very short of ammunition: the gunners desperately needed more shot, and were ready to use the plow chains and bags of scrap iron that had been sent from the shore. More of his crews were falling sick. The English fleet would have to act quickly if it was to stop the invasion.

Medina Sidonia, the Spanish commander, was very worried because he had received no news from the Duke of Parma. In the next stage of Philip's plan, the Armada was to pick up Parma's army from the Netherlands coast near Dunkirk, and escort it across the Channel to England. The Armada could not get close to the beaches because the waters around the coast were so shallow. Parma's troops would have to row several miles out to sea in barges to join the Spanish fleet.

On August 6, Medina Sidonia decided to anchor his fleet at Calais, about thirty miles from Dunkirk, until he heard from Parma. The English fleet waited nearby. The next day, a messenger from

Parma reached the Spanish fleet. He brought bad news. Parma said he needed more time to get his men ready.

There was never much chance that Parma's army could join the Spanish fleet. The Dutch rebels controlled the Netherlands coast. They had small, well-armed ships that were specially designed for sailing in shallow waters. If Parma's men tried to reach the Armada, the Dutch rebels would probably attack and kill most of them. In deeper waters, the Spanish fleet would be unable to help them. Philip had always ignored this problem when Parma pointed it out.

Before midnight on August 7 the Spanish saw strange fires blazing on the sea: fireships! The English commanders had chosen eight small ships and stuffed them with anything that would burn. Then they had set them on fire. The fireships sailed swiftly toward the Armada; their guns were firing, and sparks shot into the sky. The Spanish may have thought these were "Hellburners," exploding ships that could kill thousands. In their panic, the Spanish sea captains ordered their men to cut the anchor cables of their ships and the Armada scattered before the wind. For the first time, the English had broken the defenses of the Spanish fleet.

△ The Spanish commanders knew that fireships were the most deadly weapons. In 1585 Dutch rebels destroyed a Spanish-held bridge at Antwerp (*above*) with "Hellburners," a special type of fireship filled with bricks and gunpowder.

△ The Spanish army in the Netherlands was the best army in Europe. Philip's invasion plan could only succeed if these soldiers joined the Armada before it sailed across the Channel to England.

27

THE LAST BATTLE

△ The Spanish galleass *San Lorenzo* was damaged by an accident during the fireship attack. The English captured it early next morning.

▷ The Battle of Gravelines was the fiercest of all the battles between the two fleets. The Spanish soldiers tried to grapple and board the English ships, but even at this close range the English were still too nimble to be caught.

△ The rebel Dutch fleet captured the *San Mateo*, after the Battle of Gravelines. They took this holy banner from the ship and displayed it in triumph in Leyden Cathedral.

At dawn after the fireship attack, Medina Sidonia sent his few remaining ships to gather the Spanish fleet together. English ships chased after them through heavy seas and blustery winds. More ships had joined the English fleet it and it now easily outnumbered the Armada. Howard was now determined to fight the Spanish ships at close range. He knew this was his best chance of defeating them.

At the Battle of Gravelines, the ships came close enough for the musketeers to fire at each other and for the soldiers to exchange insults. During the battle, heavy shot smashed through the upper decks and pierced the ships' hulls. Smoke from the guns swirled all around and, as the men fought, they stumbled over fallen rigging. On all sides there were the cries of wounded men. The English and the Spanish soldiers fought with outstanding bravery in a battle which must have been both terrifying and chaotic.

After many hours, when it seemed that the Armada's crescent must break at last, the fleets were separated by a sudden rainstorm. When it passed, the English did not repeat their attack because they had run out of ammunition. The two fleets never fought again.

That night, both sides counted their losses. The Spanish had suffered most. Hundreds of their men were dead and almost all of the big fighting ships were leaking. As a strong wind drove the fleets up the North Sea, two Spanish ships sank and two were captured by rebel Dutch ships. The Dutch killed and threw the ordinary Spanish soldiers and sailors overboard, but they kept the gentlemen in the hope of getting a ransom for them.

EVENTS AT CALAIS

August 6	The two fleets anchor at Calais.
August 7	Medina Sidonia learns that Parma's army is not ready.
August 7/8	The fireship attack.
August 8	The Battle of Gravelines.
August 9	Dutch rebels capture the *San Mateo* and the *San Felipe*.

THE TERRIBLE JOURNEY

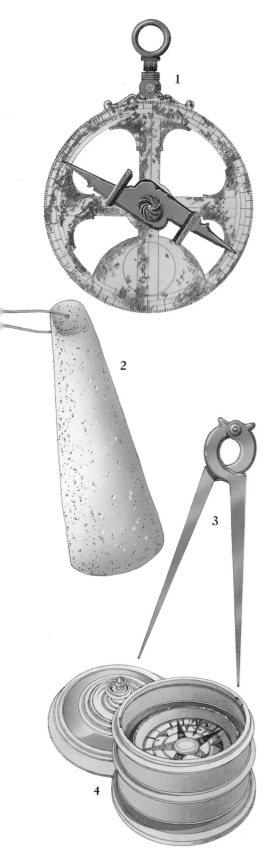

The Armada was too badly damaged to return to the Channel and fight the English fleet. Its commanders decided instead to save as many ships as they could and sail home to Spain. They chose a route around the north coast of Scotland and Ireland. Precise sailing instructions were passed to each ship with this warning: "Take great heed lest you fall upon the island of Ireland, for fear of the harm that may happen unto you upon that coast." Food and drink for each man was reduced to half a pound of biscuit, a pint of water and half a pint of wine per day. The night of August 13 was the last time the fleet stayed together. The terrible journey had begun.

Throughout the journey, the Spanish had shown they were good seamen. Now their skills were tested to the limit. Both the ships and the men had come prepared for a coastal voyage to the English Channel, not for an autumn journey into dangerous and unfamiliar seas. The cold northern mists chilled the crews who were already weakened by bad food and the shortage of water. By August 21, 3,000 men were sick.

Few of the pilots had ever seen Ireland's rocky coasts before, and they had no accurate charts to guide them. Their navigational instruments could only tell them how far north or south they were, not how far east or west. To use their instruments, the pilots needed to see the sun or the stars, but the weather here was usually cloudy. Many ships lost their way.

In the Atlantic seas around Ireland, September is always the season of gales. In 1588 the weather was exceptionally severe. Storm followed storm in a month of driving winds, crashing seas and rain. The men struggled to pump out the water that leaked into the ships' holds and to patch the leaks. Most of the Armada's ships survived and sailed on to Spain. But some were driven toward Ireland by the storms or sailed there in a desperate search for food and water. Few of these ships escaped.

By the end of September, 25 or more Spanish ships lay wrecked on the coast of Ireland. Their crews lost the only homes they had. Thousands of men drowned; an English official, who rode along one beach in the west of Ireland, reported, "I numbered in one strand of less than five miles 1,110 dead corpses of men which the sea had driven upon the shore." But the fate of the thousands who reached the shore alive was just as tragic.

◁ Every Armada ship carried an **astrolabe** (1) which helped the pilot find his position by the sun and stars. A **sounding lead** (2) measured the depth of the water. Sometimes, a little fat was fixed to it; then the sand, shingle or mud on the seabed, which stuck to the fat, might indicate to an experienced pilot the ship's position. A pair of **compasses** (3) marked the ship's route on a chart. A **compass** (4) showed the direction in which the ship was sailing.

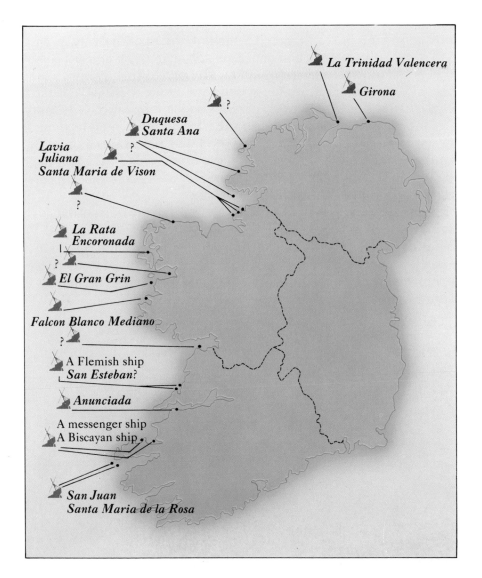

La Trinidad Valencera

Girona

Duquesa
Santa Ana

Lavia
Juliana
Santa Maria de Vison

La Rata
Encoronada

El Gran Grin

Falcon Blanco Mediano

A Flemish ship
San Esteban?

Anunciada

A messenger ship
A Biscayan ship

San Juan
Santa Maria de la Rosa

◁ The modern map of Ireland (*left*) shows the sites of Armada wrecks. The smaller chart (*above*) was the best guide available to sailors in 1588. The inaccuracy of sixteenth-century charts was one of the causes of the tragedy.

"We were fit only to die, for the wind was so strong and the sea so wild that the waves mounted to the skies, knocking the ship about so that the men were all exhausted, yet unable to keep down the water that leaked through our gaping seams. If we had not the wind astern we would not have kept afloat at all. But by God's mercy during the next two days the weather moderated, and we were able to patch up some of the leaks with ox hides and planks . . . The weather then got so strong that our poor repairs were all undone, and we had to keep both pumps always going to keep the water down. So we decided to sail for the first Scottish land even if we had to run the hulk ashore . . . During the night we gave ourselves up for lost . . . The sea kept on giving us such dreadful blows that truly our one thought was that our lives were ended, and each one of us reconciled himself to God as well as he could, and prepared for the long journey that seemed inevitable . . . So we gave way to despair . . . and we looked towards the land with full eyes and hearts, as the reader may imagine. And God send that he may be able to imagine the smallest part of what it was like, for after all there is a great difference between those who suffer and those who look upon suffering from afar."

This account of the storms of autumn 1588 was written by a survivor from the wreck of the *Gran Grifon* on Fair Isle.

THE SPANISH IN IRELAND

An English army first conquered Ireland in the twelfth century. In 1588 it was still a strange and dangerous place to the English soldiers and officials who governed it. The native Irish people were mostly Catholics, not Protestants, and they spoke their own Gaelic language, not English. A group of rebel lords in the north of Ireland were the greatest threat to English rule. These lords lived in stone towers and had their own fighting men. The English were afraid that the Spanish survivors would join the rebel lords and defeat the small English army. The Queen's Lord Deputy ordered his officers to catch and kill all Spaniards.

During the next few weeks the Spanish survivors must often have wished they were back on their filthy, disease-ridden ships. Under stormy autumn skies, the English soldiers hunted them like animals. Sometimes the Irish people helped the Spanish, but often they robbed them and stripped them naked, or handed them over to the English. Then death was certain.

▽ Three Spanish ships were wrecked in Streedagh Bay, Sligo. The men who came ashore were cold, sick and hungry after four months at sea. They were stripped and robbed by the Irish. When night came, the survivors covered themselves with grass to keep warm, and they watched wolves and crows eat the bodies on the beach.

In Mayo, one Irish fighter boasted that he had killed 80 men in a day with his ax. He was probably in the pay of the English government. In Galway the English took 300 Spanish prisoners to a monastery and killed them in front of the local people. The Spanish could not even surrender to save their lives. The 450 survivors of one Spanish ship, the *Trinidad Valencera*, were promised their lives by a group of English soldiers. But when the men put down their guns they were stripped and killed.

Should the English be blamed for these murders? They were outnumbered by the Spanish soldiers who came ashore in Ireland and they were afraid that they would be overrun by them. The Spanish would probably have done the same if English soldiers had landed in one of their colonies. But it is hard to justify the murder of a group of Dutch boys who had been forced to join the Armada against their will and who had survived the wrecks.

TO SAFETY IN SCOTLAND

How could the Spanish survivors escape from Ireland when all their ships had been wrecked? They must have despaired of ever seeing Spain again. Then came the news that seemed like a miracle. A magnificent galleass, the *Girona*, had survived the storms and was being repaired in Killybegs harbor. The harbor was controlled by a rebel Irish lord, and was a place of safety for the Spanish. Full of hope, hundreds of men walked many miles to join the ship.

The *Girona* was too badly damaged to sail to Spain, so the officers decided to sail it to Scotland instead. The Scots were not involved in the war between England and Spain, and might help the Spanish soldiers get home. For two days the ship struggled around the northern coast of Ireland. Soon it was in trouble. Its timbers creaked loudly, then the rudder broke and the ship began to lurch and roll dangerously in the heavy seas. In the middle of the night, a hidden rock ripped open the ship's hull. Guns, ammunition, food, treasure and 1,300 men all tumbled into the sea. In ten minutes the tragedy was over. The *Girona*, the last Armada ship in Ireland, broke to pieces and was gone. Only nine men survived. Luckily, they came ashore in Ireland near the castle of a great rebel lord, Sorley Boy McDonnell. He was already protecting several hundred Spanish soldiers from the English army, and he sent them all to Scotland in his own ships.

One historian has calculated that, in all, between 6,000 and 7,000 men were shipwrecked off the Irish coast. Of these, about 4,000 were drowned, 1,500 were killed by the English and 750 reached Scotland.

The same Atlantic storms that drove Armada ships on to the coast of Ireland forced back the supply ship, the *Gran Grifon*, to the north of Scotland. It ran ashore on Fair Isle. The captain, Gomez de Medina, and his men found only 17 families on the whole island where they lived off fish and barley meal bread. The men could have easily killed the islanders and taken their food. Instead, Captain Medina paid well for everything the islanders could spare, and waited to be rescued by the Scots.

A ship on its way to the Shetland Islands eventually picked up the Spanish. From there they took another ship to the mainland of Scotland. By December 1588 *Gran Grifon* survivors reached the Scottish capital, Edinburgh, where the leading Catholic lords gave them a warm welcome. They were so weak from hunger and illness that they could hardly walk. King James VI of Scotland gave all the survivors a safe passage home. Captain Medina never forgot the kindness of the Scots. On his return to Cadiz he found a Scottish ship which was being held under arrest. Medina went to Philip and obtained its release. He then sent it back to Scotland with his greetings.

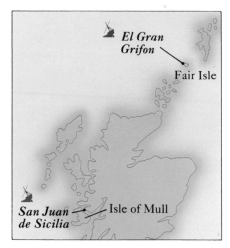

△ Two Spanish ships were wrecked on Scottish islands. The *San Juan de Sicilia* exploded mysteriously on the Isle of Mull. The English government claimed that one of its spies blew it up, but this has never been proven.

△ The Spanish repaired the galleass
Girona at Killybegs harbor. They used
timbers and fittings from another
Spanish ship that was beached nearby.
The local Irish lord gave them horses
for food and received wine and muskets
in return.

EVIDENCE FROM THE WRECKS

The objects on the following pages have all been found in the last 20 years. They were recovered from Armada wrecks in Ireland by underwater archeologists, who often had to work in very dangerous waters. These discoveries are particularly exciting because they reveal so much about the lives of the ordinary soldiers and sailors who took part in the voyage.

Study of the wrecks has changed the way historians think about the Armada. For a long time they believed that the Spanish ships had run out of ammunition by the end of the journey. Now it is clear that the Armada had plenty of ammunition because so much gunpowder and shot has been found on the wrecks. There are other surprises. The gaming cups, shown here, reveal that the men sometimes disobeyed Medina Sidonia's order forbidding them to gamble.

The most precious items on these pages were found on board the wreck of the *Girona*. There were many young noblemen on board this ship, who had hoped to win wealth and honor in the invasion of England. They had brought with them chests full of fine clothes, jewelry, gold and silver. The evidence from the wrecks also shows very clearly the contrast between the lives of the wealthy gentlemen and the common crew. The crew ate their food with simple spoons from wooden bowls, while the gentlemen used fine plates, goblets and forks made of gold, silver and pewter.

We can imagine the sadness that was felt by the friends and relatives of the dead men when we look at these personal possessions. Divers found a ring on the wreck of the *Girona* that was probably given by a girl to her lover before he left Spain. It is decorated with a hand holding a heart and has the inscription in Spanish, "I have nothing more to give you."

The men knew the dangers they faced from sickness and shipwreck on a long voyage like this, and they wore crucifixes and other religious objects to protect them. This time the protection had failed.

▷ **Findings from Armada wrecks**
1. Bosun's silver whistle.
2. Dagger.
3. Wooden gaming cups.
4. Wooden bowl and spoon.
5. Bronze mortar (in which to pound food and medicines).
6. Pewter invalid bowl.
On the next page:
7. Silver candlesticks.
8. Gold pendant in the shape of a salamander.
9. Pewter plate.
10. Silver perfume bottle with crystal stopper.
11. Gold cross of a knight of Santiago.
12. Gold and silver coins.
13. A small gold box (which contained holy objects).
14. Silver fork.
15. Gold tooth-and earpick.
16. Gold rings.
17. Gold cross of a knight of Malta.
18. Cameo of a Roman emperor.

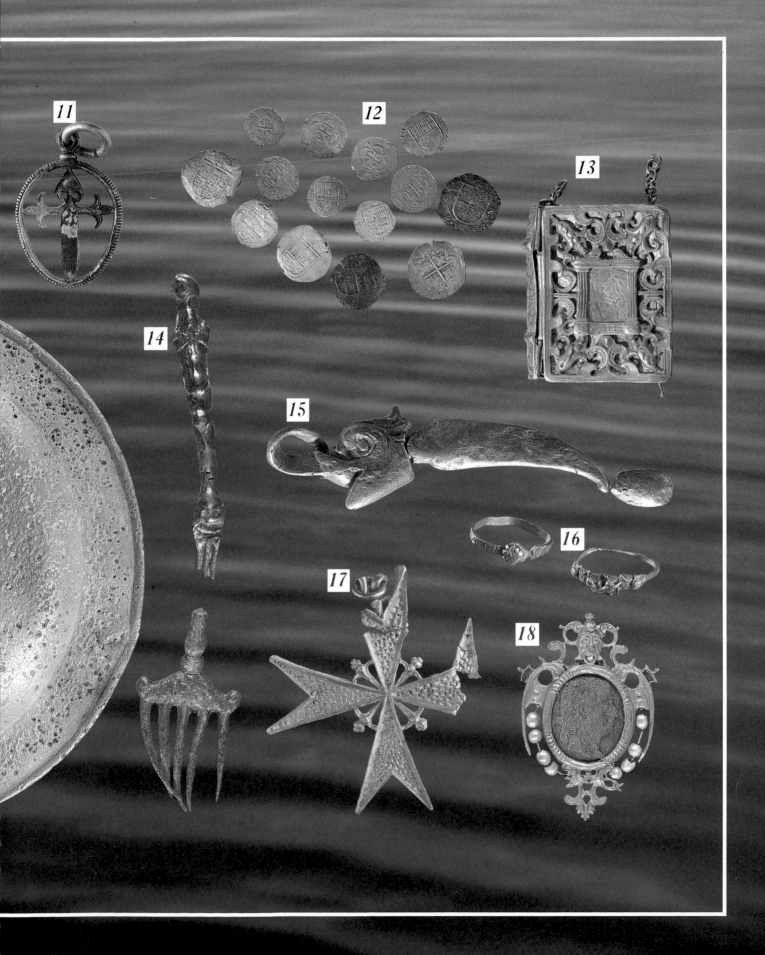

AFTER THE ARMADA

△ After the Armada campaign there was no money to help wounded and needy sailors. In 1590 Hawkins, Howard and Drake started a fund for this purpose. The money came from the sailors themselves. Sixpence a month was taken from the sailors' wages. It was kept in a locked chest at Chatham dockyard. Because the first Chatham Chest was robbed so often, a stronger one (*above*) was made.

▷ Two pictures from a seventeenth-century English deck of cards. The cards tell the story of the Armada from the English point of view. One card (*left*) shows Spanish sorrow at the return to Spain of the shattered Spanish fleet. The other (*right*) shows Elizabeth's victory procession to St. Paul's Cathedral in November 1588.

About 90 Armada ships returned to Spain in the autumn of 1588. Their crews suffered terribly during the voyage home. Some ships had no food, others had no water and the men's clothes were in rags. The local people at the Spanish ports of San Sebastian, Santander and Corunna gave the men money and food, but it was not enough. Weeks passed before medical help was provided. Some of the men had to stay on their ships because there was nowhere else to go. The Spanish commander, Medina Sidonia, was too ill to sit up, and he wrote to Philip that he would rather die than go to sea again. Many people unfairly blamed Medina Sidonia for the disaster. As he traveled back to his home, in Cadiz, children threw stones at his carriage. Nearly every noble family in Spain had lost a father, a son or another close relative. The whole of Spain went into mourning.

In the ports of both England and Spain, seamen lay in the streets, sick and half-naked. They could not buy food or clothes because their wages had not been paid. They had fought against each other only two months earlier. Now it hardly mattered to them which country had won or lost. Men continued to die, months after the last sea battle. In Spain, people blamed bakers for putting lime in the flour. In England, sailors blamed brewers for making sour beer. No one realized that the deaths were due to diseases spread by dirt and vermin and by sailors wearing dead men's clothes. In the end, up to half the men in the English fleet and two thirds of the men in the Spanish fleet lost their lives.

The Spaniards bewailing ye misfortune of their friends

Queene Eliz: Riding in Triumph through London in a Chariot drawn by two Horses and all ye Companies attending her with their Baners

◁ The soldiers and sailors who survived the Armada campaign joined other poor people on the roads of England. Many of them lived by begging or stealing food and money.

△ Many medals like this one were made in England in 1588 to celebrate the victory over the Spanish Armada. The English government may have given them to officers in the English fleet, as a reward for their services to the country.

The English government was very relieved when, in late September 1588, it heard about the Spanish wrecks off Ireland. There was now no chance of a Spanish invasion that year. All over the country, church bells were rung in celebration and town councils held public dinners. In December 1588 Elizabeth went in procession to St Paul's Cathedral. As always, the Queen dressed richly in fine clothes and jewels, and she rode in a chariot through streets which were packed with cheering crowds. Houses were decorated with banners and garlands of flowers. Elizabeth believed that the Spanish invasion had failed because God had supported the Protestants. In the ceremony at St Paul's, banners that had been captured from Spanish ships were hung in the cathedral and Elizabeth gave thanks to God for the great English victory.

The Armada campaign cost both Spain and England a great deal of money and a great many lives. This did not stop Philip and Elizabeth from continuing the war. In 1589 Drake led an English fleet in an attack on Portugal, which was part of the Spanish empire. This expedition was a total failure and led to Drake's disgrace. After further attacks on one another, which continued until the end of the century, England and Spain finally signed a peace treaty in 1604. By then, both Philip and Elizabeth were dead.

THE ARMADA MYTH

△ Elizabeth's Armada portrait, pictures of the fireship attack and the Irish storms. English people liked to believe that God sent the winds that helped to destroy the Armada.

▽ In this English painting, the crescent-shaped Armada is shown as a dragon. Its defeat is seen as a victory of good over evil.

How important was the Armada campaign? It is certainly one of the most exciting and dramatic stories in European history. The common men and commanders on both sides showed great skill, courage and endeavor. But the Armada campaign was just one event in a long war between England and Spain. It settled nothing. In the long term the defeat of the Armada did not weaken Spain. On the contrary, the country grew richer and its navy became more powerful. Nor did the Armada's failure lead to the triumph of England and the Protestants over Spain and the Catholics. In truth, neither side was strong enough to defeat the other, but it took them many years to realize the fact.

Spanish people remember the Armada against England as just one of several armadas during Philip's reign. Some armadas, such as the one against the Turks at Lepanto, were successful; the one against England was not. Its defeat wounded Spanish pride, but it was only a temporary setback.

Why, then, do English people celebrate 1588 as if it were such an important date? The answer lies not in historical truth, but in myths – in other words, what people like to believe happened rather than what actually *did* happen.

The myths about the Armada began with the propaganda that was published by the English government in 1588. The government wanted to stir up patriotism among its people and encourage hatred of the Spanish. Then, as now, governments knew

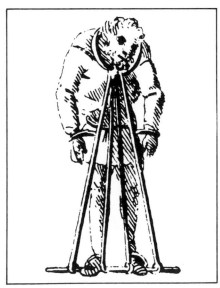

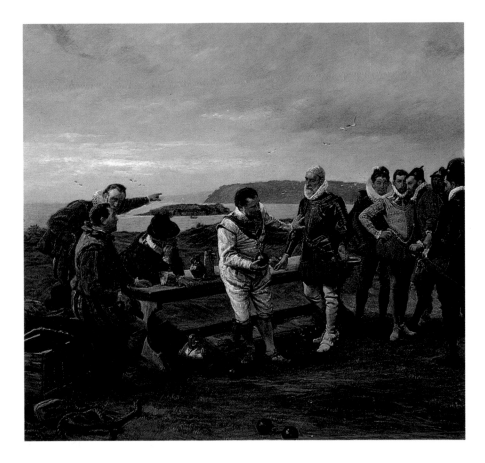

In the reign of Queen Victoria, the English made Drake a national hero. This nineteenth-century painting illustrates an old story that Drake was playing bowls when the Armada was first spotted. In the story, Drake says, "We have time enough to finish the game and beat the Spanish too." There is little evidence that the story is true. Both the story and the painting were popular because they made Drake seem brave and confident in the face of danger.

that words were important weapons. So, in 1588, English officials published a letter which, they said, was found in the room of a Catholic priest. In fact the letter was probably forged by Lord Burghley, one of Elizabeth's ministers. The letter said that the Spanish ships carried nooses to hang English people, and iron brands to mark the faces of all young children. It said that Medina Sidonia was such a coward that he had hidden in the hold of his ship during the Armada battles. These were deliberate lies, as the government well knew. The letter also said that the English fleet captured and sank a large number of Spanish ships. This too was nonsense. But it was out of propaganda like this that the Armada myth was born.

In England, people liked to believe that the Armada failed because the English were a superior nation and because God was on their side. In later centuries, when the country was again threatened with invasion, the memory of the great victory over the Spanish Armada (as they believed) comforted English people and gave them courage.

But myths can be harmful. We must look at the event with fresh eyes and avoid bias in favor of either England or Spain. The result is an Armada story that is very different from the one the English often believe.

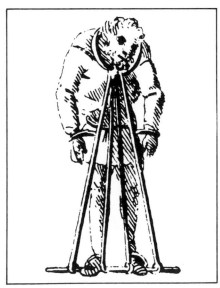

△ "The Scavenger's Daughter" was a torture instrument that bent and pressed the victim's body. For centuries it was displayed in the Tower of London as a Spanish torture instrument taken from the Armada. It is almost certainly English.

GLOSSARY

alliance   A pact made between two countries or families to look after their mutual interests.

archeologist   A person who studies history by examining buried remains, such as houses, ships, pottery, tools, and weapons.

arquebus   A type of gun used by soldiers in the sixteenth century. It was fired from the shoulder like a rifle.

astrolabe   A navigational instrument used by sailors to measure the angle of the sun or a star above the horizon. It showed sailors how far north or south their ship was.

barrel   The long, tube-shaped part of a gun.

beacon   A fire which people placed on a hill to give warning. The fire was often placed on a pole in an iron cage.

bias   A feeling for or against something without knowing enough facts to be able to judge fairly.

brand   An iron stamp for burning a mark on a person or an animal to show who owns it.

campaign   An organized military attack.

chart   A map for sailors that shows coasts, rocks and other features in the sea.

civil war   A war between people of the same country.

coat-of-arms   A symbol used by a family as their special sign.

colony   A country or area which is owned and controlled by another country.

compass   A navigational instrument used by sailors to find the direction in which their ship is sailing. The needle of the compass will always point to magnetic North.

compasses   A V-shaped instrument with two pointed arms. Sailors used it for measuring distances on maps or charts.

convoy   A group of merchant ships that are protected by fighting ships.

ducat   A gold or silver coin that was once used in many places in Europe.

dysentery   A painful disease that causes severe diarrhea with bleeding.

empire   A number of countries that are owned and controlled by another country.

envoy   An official messenger who is sent by one government to do business with another.

flagship   The most important ship in a squadron. It has a special flag to show when the admiral is on board.

grappling hook   A large metal hook on the end of a pole. Sailors used grappling hooks to pull an enemy ship alongside.

gun carriage   A heavy wooden frame on wheels, on which a gun was placed.

hold   The space at the bottom of a ship where the supplies are carried.

hull   The sides and bottom of a ship.

interest   A sum of money paid for a loan. A high rate of interest means that the payment is greater.

invest   When you invest money, you hope to make more money because the thing you buy will increase in value.

merchant ship   A ship that carried goods for trade. They were often well armed, even in peacetime, to protect them from attack.

militia   A group of men who are trained to serve as soldiers if their country is attacked. They do not belong to a regular army.

musket   A type of gun that was used by soldiers (musketeers). It was heavier than the arquebus, but a lot more powerful. Soldiers rested it on a forked support when it was fired.

myth   A false story that a lot of people believe.

navigation   The art of finding a ship's position and the direction in which it is sailing, in order to take it safely to its destination.

patriotism   Love for one's country.

persecution   Persecution is making people suffer, often for religious or political reasons.

pike   A weapon which was carried by a soldier. It was a long, wooden pole with a metal point at the end.

pilot   Someone who has been specially trained to navigate a ship.

policy   A plan of action which has been chosen by a government.

powder   Powder (gunpowder) was a dry explosive mixture that was used to fire a gun.

press   To force men to join the army or navy.

privateers   Sailors with official documents from their governments who attacked and captured the merchant ships of other countries.

propaganda   Biased information which is spread by a government in order to influence people's opinions.

rebel   When citizens rebel, they fight against the government that rules them.

rigging   Ropes that were used on ships to support the masts and to raise and lower the sails.

rudder   A long, flat piece of wood which is fixed to the back (stern) of a ship and steers it through the water.

scurvy   A disease caused by lack of Vitamin C. First the gums swell up and the teeth fall out. Then large blotches appear on the skin. In the past, sailors often got scurvy because they had no fresh fruit or vegetables in their diet.

ships' biscuit   Ships' biscuit was an important part of a sailor's diet. It was made from flour and water and was shaped into flat cakes. It was baked slowly until it was very hard and dry.

shot   Heavy balls of stone or metal which were fired from guns.

siege gun   A large gun on a gun carriage. It was used to attack castles and towns.

sounding lead   A heavy piece of lead which was tied to a rope, and dropped into the sea to measure the depth of water.

squadron   A group of fighting ships.

stalemate   A conflict which neither side can win.

taper   A piece of string which is covered with wax. In sea battles, a taper was lit and used to set fire to the powder in a gun.

touch hole   A small hole which was filled with powder, on the side of the gun barrel. The powder in the touch hole was lit with a taper. This lit the powder inside the gun and made the gun fire.

treason   To work for the enemies of your country is an act of treason.

treaty   A signed agreement between countries.

typhus   An infectious disease carried by lice and fleas. It makes red spots appear on the body and causes a fever.

victuals   Food and drink.

wadding   A bundle of cloth which was packed into the barrel of a gun. It kept the powder and shot in place before the gun was fired.

worms   The grubs of a small beetle called a weevil. The grubs infested the grain and ships' biscuit that the sailors ate.

INDEX

PRINTED IN BELGIUM BY
proost
INTERNATIONAL BOOK PRODUCTION